It's all about . . .

HORSES
AND FOALS

KINGFISHER
LONDON & NEW YORK

KINGFISHER
LONDON & NEW YORK

Copyright © Macmillan Publishers International Ltd 2018
Published in the United States by Kingfisher,
175 Fifth Ave., New York, NY 10010
Kingfisher is an imprint of Macmillan Children's Books, London
All rights reserved.

Distributed in the U.S. and Canada by Macmillan,
175 Fifth Ave., New York, NY 10010

Library of Congress Cataloging-in-Publication data
has been applied for.

Series editor: Sarah Snashall
Series design: Anthony Hannant (Little Red Ant)
Written by Sarah Snashall

ISBN: 978-0-7534-7412-9

Kingfisher books are available for special promotions
and premiums. For details contact: Special Markets
Department, Macmillan, 175 Fifth Ave.,
New York, NY 10010.

For more information, please visit
www.kingfisherbooks.com

Printed in China

9 8 7 6 5 4 3 2 1

1TR/1017/WKT/UG/105MA

Picture credits
The Publisher would like to thank the following for permission to reproduce their material.
Top = t; Bottom = b; Center = c; Left = l; Right = r
Cover iStock/mari_art; back cover iStock/Callipso; Pages 2–3, 30–31 iStock/fotoVoyager;
4 iStock/USO; 5t Shutterstock/Christos Geroghiou; 5b iStock/cgbadaulf; 6–7 iStock/
Abramova_ksenlya; 8 Alamy/Zuzana Buráƌová; 9t Alamy/Trinity Mirror/Mirrorpix;
9b iStock/akabel; 10 iStock/dennisvdw; 11t Shutterstock/pirita; 11b Getty/Barcroft;
12 iStock/Seppfriedhuber; 13t iStock/dgphotography; 13c Alamy/Juniors Bildarchiv
GmbH; 13b iStock/Lorado; 14 iStock/Byrdyak; 15t Shutterstock/Lenkaden; 15b iStock/
Nigeldowsett; 16 Getty/Peter Bischoff/Stringer; 17 iStock/Geogijevic; 17b iStock/
virogonira; 18 iStock/scigelova; 19 Alamy/dpa picture alliance; 20–21 iStock/marienka;
20 Getty/Focus on sport; 21t Alamy/Kim Peterson; 22 Alamy/alandawsonphotography;
23c iStock/coolphotography; 23b Getty/Hulton Deutsch; 24 Shutterstock/Fotokostic;
25t iStock/SasahFoxWalters; 25 & 26 Shutterstock/Fotokostic; 27t & c Anthony Hannant;
27b Getty/Michele Westmorland; 28 Alamy BSIP SA; 29 iStock/Rosette Jordaan; 29b Alamy/
Agencja Fotograficzna Caro; 32 Shutterstock/mariait.
Cards: Front tl iStock/Stocknshares; tr Shutterstock/mariait; bl Shutterstock/Marina
Kondratenko; br iStock/Somogyvari; Back tl iStock/kondakov; tr Shutterstock/loflo69;
bl Shutterstock/Martin Fowler; br iStock/andyworks.

Front cover: This foal has a thick white stripe, or blaze, down the middle of its face.

CONTENTS

Magnificent horses

People have lived and worked with horses for about 5000 years. Before cars and tractors, horses were the most important form of transportation. Today, horses are kept for riding, racing, and companionship, as well as for work in many parts of the world.

Horses are beautiful and intelligent.

Pegasus, the Greek winged horse, was a symbol of wisdom.

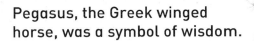

FACT ...

Rhinoceroses and tapirs are the closest relatives to the horse family.

SPOTLIGHT: Incitatus

Famous for:	Caligula's beloved horse, said to have lived in a marble stable
Breed:	unknown
Owned by:	Emperor Caligula, Ancient Rome

Horses like to live together. A group of horses is called a herd.

A horse's body

Horses and ponies are powerful animals. They are measured in "hands." A horse is usually more than 14.3 hands; a pony is less than 14.3 hands.

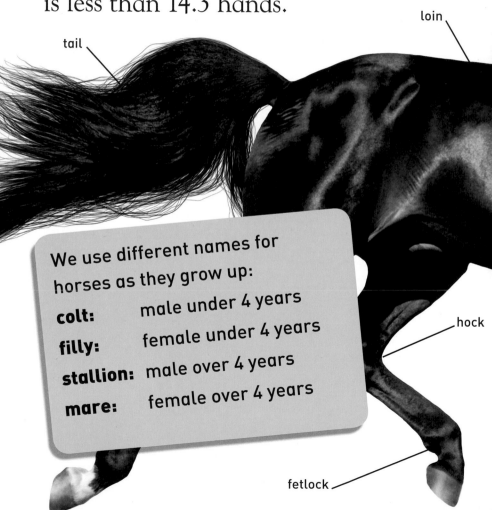

loin

tail

hock

fetlock

We use different names for horses as they grow up:

colt: male under 4 years

filly: female under 4 years

stallion: male over 4 years

mare: female over 4 years

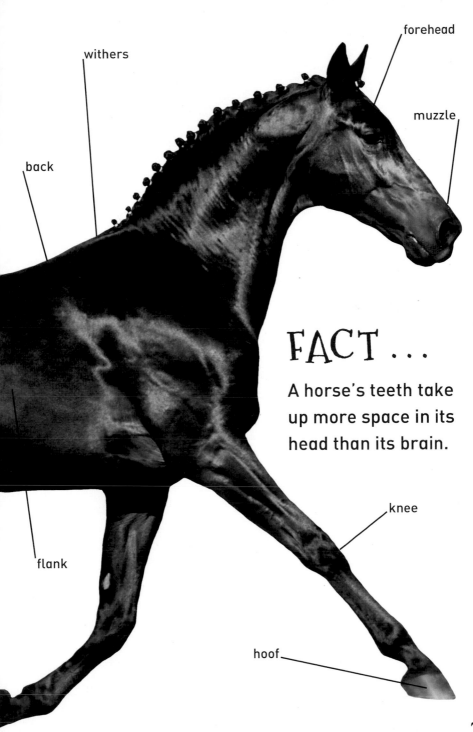

forehead

withers

muzzle

back

FACT...

A horse's teeth take up more space in its head than its brain.

knee

flank

hoof

Fast and strong

There are hundreds of different breeds of horse and pony. Different breeds have different abilities. Thoroughbreds and Arabs are good at racing and jumping. Shire horses and Percherons are good at pulling plows and carriages.

Appaloosas are strong, fast horses with unusual spotted markings.

FACT ...

A horse has bigger eyes than any other land animal.

SPOTLIGHT: Red Rum

Famous for:	champion steeplechaser, who won the Grand National three times
Breed:	thoroughbred
Owned by:	Noel Le Mare, Southport, England

Strong shire horses compete in plowing competitions.

What is a pony?

A pony is a short horse. Ponies have a shorter head and legs, a thicker neck and a longer mane and tail. Wild ponies have lived for thousands of years on British moorlands.

Wild ponies live in groups of about 20 ponies. One pony will be the lead pony.

FACT ...

Exmoor ponies have an oily waterproof coat and especially thick eyelids to keep water out of their eyes.

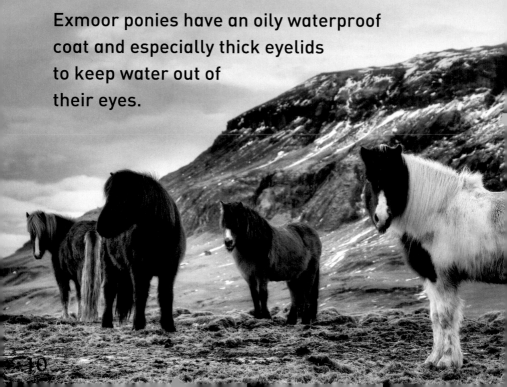

Many children learn to ride on a pony.

SPOTLIGHT: Thumbelina

Famous for:	being the smallest horse in the world; just 17 inches (43cm) tall
Breed:	miniature horse
Owner:	Paul & Kay Goessling, St Louis

Horses around the world

Horses are loved and celebrated across the world at sporting events and festivals. Many nomadic people still live a life centered on their horses.

FACT ...

There are more horses in Mongolia than there are people.

At a rodeo, cowboys practice their horse-riding skills.

Indian Marwari horses wear tack that is decorated with silver, jewels, and bells.

Polo is a team sport played on horses. The game was invented in Persia (modern Iran) 2500 years ago.

Foals

Most baby foals are born at night. Within an hour the foal will be able to stand and feed. In a few hours it will be able to trot. When a foal is a year old, it becomes a yearling.

A foal's legs are almost as long as they will be when it is an adult.

FACT ...

A foal can gallop when it is just one day old.

A foal and its mother use their sense of smell to recognize each other.

15

Getting to know you

Horses are sociable animals that live in groups in the wild. They use nickers, neighing, and nostril blowing to talk to each other. Horses form bonds with humans by smelling us, hearing us talk gently, or by being stroked.

Special trainers, known as horse whisperers, are skilled at communicating with horses.

Horses and ponies groom and nip each other to make friends.

FACT ...

A horse has 10 muscles in each ear. Their ears can be moved precisely to hear particular sounds.

A horse's ears can be pricked forward (interested), or back (angry), or can twitch (relaxed).

17

Jumping and dressage

Horses and their riders can compete in many ways: at gymkhanas, shows, show jumping, and dressage events. Riders can demonstrate how well they can control their horse, how good it looks, or how high it can jump.

Horses jump over different obstacles at a show-jumping competition.

British horse Valegro won gold medals at the 2012 and 2016 Olympics.

In a dressage competition, a rider must lead the horse through a number of special moves—a bit like dancing.

SPOTLIGHT: Valegro

Famous for:	being a world record-breaking Olympic dressage winner
Breed:	thoroughbred
Rider:	Charlotte Dujardin, England

Racing

Horses can naturally run very fast to escape from predators in the wild. People have bred the fastest horses to create champion racehorses.

Secretariat won many races in 1972 and 1973.

At the end of a race, horses gallop almost 30 miles (48 kilometers) per hour!

FACT ...

The horses competing in Italy's Palio are taken into church before the race to receive a blessing.

The Palio race in Siena, Italy, takes place around the town square.

SPOTLIGHT: Secretariat

Famous for:	being one of the greatest American racehorses of all time
Breed:	thoroughbred
Owned by:	Meadow Stable, Virginia

21

Hard at work

Tractors and cars have replaced much of a horse's work, but we still need some hardworking horses. Police officers on horseback can see more clearly than police on foot or in a vehicle.

Mounted police officers can help to protect crowds.

Horses are still used to round up livestock on farms. Soldiers no longer go into battle on horseback, but they often still ride horses on parade or when on guard.

FACT ...

The Navajo tribe uses horses to herd sheep and goats in the Sonoran Desert, USA.

Horses in the First World War wore gas masks when under a gas attack.

Saddles and bridles

You need to use special equipment— called tack—on a horse or pony so that you can ride safely. A saddle keeps the rider comfortable and the bridle helps the rider to "tell" the horse what to do.

saddle

bridle

bit

stirrups

girth strap

You have to clean your tack after each time you ride your horse.

FACT ...

Training a horse to be ridden is called "breaking in."

A lunge rope is used to teach a horse how to follow commands.

Trots and gallops

Horses have four main riding speeds, called paces or gaits: walking, trotting, cantering, and galloping. The rider uses different leg and rein positions to tell the horse which pace to use.

A horse nods its head as it walks along.

1

2

A trot can feel bumpy and the rider can rise up in the saddle.

A canter is a three-beat pace, which means you can hear three hoof beats per stride.

3

4

When a horse gallops, all four hooves come off the ground at the same time.

Caring for your horse

A horse can be kept in a field or a stable, but it will be happier with other horses. Your horse will need the right food, clean water, and plenty of exercise to stay clean and healthy.

A horse or pony should be groomed after every ride.

You need to clean out your horse's stable regularly and put down fresh bedding.

A farrier removes a horse's old shoes, trims its hooves, and puts on new shoes.

GLOSSARY

bedding Straw used on the floor of a stable.

breaking in Training a horse to be ridden.

breed A group of animals that look the same.

bridle The straps and buckles that go around a horse's head.

celebrated Given awards and talked about.

dressage A sport in which a rider controls their horse to carry out complicated movements.

farrier Someone who takes care of and fits metal shoes to a horse's hooves.

gait The way a horse moves.

grooming Brushing and cleaning a horse's hair and checking its hooves for pebbles.

gymkhana A horse show, often for children, with jumping, games, and racing.

hands A measurement for saying how tall a horse is.

herd A group of horses.

intelligent Smart.

livestock Farm animals, such as sheep and cows.

markings Marks in a horse's hair.

moorland An area of land that is open and wet.

nickers A soft neighing sound made by horses.

nomadic Describes people who travel from place to place and have no fixed place they call home.

predator An animal that hunts other animals for food.

relative In the same family.

rodeo An American horse-riding sport.

saddle A shaped, padded seat that goes on a horse's back for the rider to sit on.

tack The pieces of equipment used in horse riding.

INDEX